PITTSBURGH STEELERS

BY WILL GRAVES

SportsZone

An Imprint of Abdo Publishing
abdopublishing.com

abdopublishing.com

Published by Abdo Publishing, a division of ABDO, PO Box 398166, Minneapolis, Minnesota 55439. Copyright © 2017 by Abdo Consulting Group, Inc. International copyrights reserved in all countries. No part of this book may be reproduced in any form without written permission from the publisher. SportsZone™ is a trademark and logo of Abdo Publishing.

Printed in the United States of America, North Mankato, Minnesota
042016
092016

Cover Photo: Don Wright/AP Images
Interior Photos: Don Wright/AP Images, 1; NFL Photos/AP Images, 4-5, 11, 18-19; Harry Cabluck/AP Images, 6-7; Walter Stein/AP Images, 8-9; AP Images, 10, 14; Fred Kaufman/AP Images, 12-13; Vernon Biever/AP Images, 15; Paul Spinelli/AP Images, 16-17; Gene J. Puskar/AP Images, 20-21; Mark Humphrey/AP Images, 22-23; Mark J. Terrill/AP Images, 24; Chuck Burton/AP Images, 25; Mel Evans/AP Images, 26; John Bazemore/AP Images, 27; Amy Sancetta/AP Images, 28; Al Messerschmidt/AP Images, 29

Editor: Patrick Donnelly
Series Designer: Nikki Farinella

Cataloging-in-Publication Data
Names: Graves, Will, author.
Title: Pittsburgh Steelers / by Will Graves.
Description: Minneapolis, MN : Abdo Publishing, [2017] | Series: NFL up close | Includes index.
Identifiers: LCCN 2015960440 | ISBN 9781680782301 (lib. bdg.) | ISBN 9781680776416 (ebook)
Subjects: LCSH: Pittsburgh Steelers (Football team)--History--Juvenile literature. | National Football League--Juvenile literature. | Football--Juvenile literature. | Professional sports--Juvenile literature. | Football teams--Pennsylvania--Juvenile literature.
Classification: DDC 796.332--dc23
LC record available at http://lccn.loc.gov/2015960440

TABLE OF CONTENTS

FRANCO TO THE RESCUE

The Pittsburgh Steelers were in serious trouble. The Oakland Raiders had taken a 7-6 lead with just over a minute to go in their 1972 playoff game. The Steelers got the ball back for one last shot. They needed a miracle. Running back Franco Harris provided one.

Pittsburgh had the ball at its own 40-yard line with 22 seconds left. It was fourth down. Quarterback Terry Bradshaw threw the ball downfield. Raiders safety Jack Tatum smashed into Steelers running back John Fuqua as the pass arrived. The ball fluttered toward the ground near Oakland's 40-yard line.

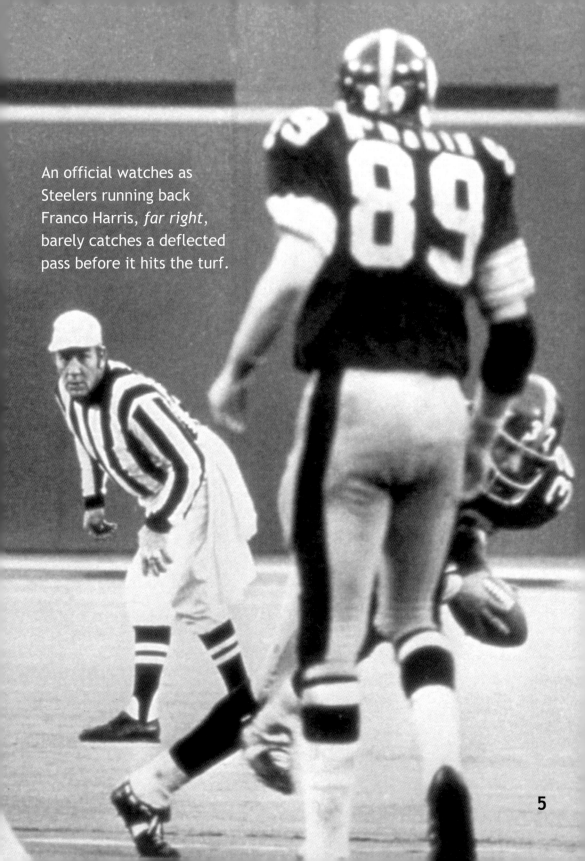

An official watches as Steelers running back Franco Harris, *far right*, barely catches a deflected pass before it hits the turf.

Then it happened. Out of nowhere, Harris scooped up the ball just before it fell incomplete. He then outraced the Raiders to the end zone. Steelers fans in Three Rivers Stadium erupted while the officials tried to determine if the play was legal. Under the rules at the time, if the ball had touched Fuqua last, Harris's catch would have been illegal.

The officials ruled the ball had bounced off Tatum last. The touchdown counted. The Steelers had pulled out a 13-7 victory thanks to one of the most famous plays in National Football League (NFL) history. It became known as "The Immaculate Reception."

It was the perfect ending for the Steelers and the start of an era of success no team has matched.

FAST FACT
The win over the Raiders was the Steelers' first playoff victory in their 40-year history.

Franco Harris outruns Oakland's Jimmy Warren as he dashes to the end zone with the winning touchdown in Pittsburgh's 1972 playoff victory.

Steelers owner Art Rooney Sr., *left*,
confers with NFL commissioner
8 Bert Bell in 1947.

HUMBLE BEGINNINGS

In 1933, Art Rooney Sr. paid $2,500 to the NFL to start a football team in Pittsburgh. The man known as "The Chief" called his team the Pirates. He switched the nickname to "Steelers" before the 1940 season to honor Pittsburgh's deep roots in the steel industry.

The Steelers were not as successful as the steel industry, however. They spent most of their first 39 years as one of the worst teams in the league. They made the playoffs only once in that span, losing to the Philadelphia Eagles in 1947.

FAST FACT

The Steelers shared Forbes Field with baseball's Pittsburgh Pirates from 1933 to 1963. They also played at the University of Pittsburgh football stadium from 1958 to 1969.

The Steelers did not have a great eye for talent in those days, especially at quarterback. They cut Pittsburgh native Johnny Unitas, who went on to a Hall of Fame career with the Baltimore Colts. They did the same with Jack Kemp and Len Dawson, quarterbacks who later won championships with the Buffalo Bills and Kansas City Chiefs, respectively.

By the end of the 1960s, Rooney was running out of patience. In 1969, he hired Chuck Noll, who was an assistant coach with the Baltimore Colts. At his first press conference, Noll said, "We'll change history." And that is exactly what happened.

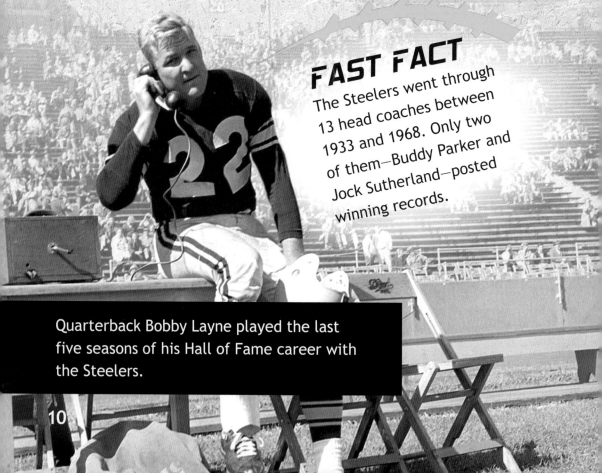

FAST FACT
The Steelers went through 13 head coaches between 1933 and 1968. Only two of them—Buddy Parker and Jock Sutherland—posted winning records.

Quarterback Bobby Layne played the last five seasons of his Hall of Fame career with the Steelers.

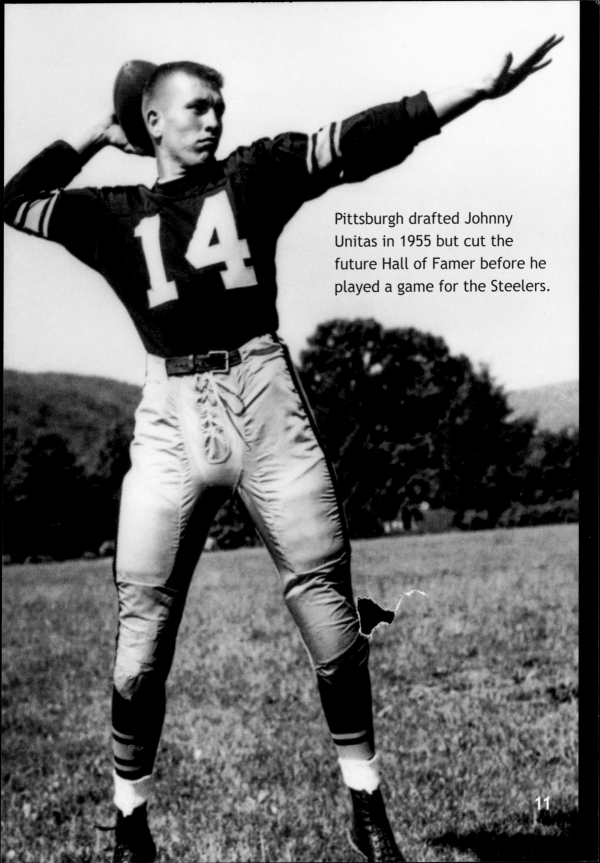

Pittsburgh drafted Johnny Unitas in 1955 but cut the future Hall of Famer before he played a game for the Steelers.

With the help of high draft picks such as "Mean" Joe Greene, 75, the Steelers slowly built a dynasty in Pittsburgh.

THE SUPER 70s

Chuck Noll got plenty of help in turning the Steelers around. Pittsburgh built itself into a contender through the NFL Draft. Over a six-year period, the Steelers drafted—and held onto—nine future Hall of Fame players.

They took defensive tackle "Mean" Joe Greene in the first round in 1969. In 1970, they selected quarterback Terry Bradshaw and safety Mel Blount. They grabbed linebacker Jack Ham in 1971 and running back Franco Harris the following year. In 1974, wide receivers John Stallworth and Lynn Swann, linebacker Jack Lambert, and center Mike Webster joined the team through the draft.

FAST FACT

Art Rooney's first choice for coach in 1969 was Penn State's Joe Paterno. He turned down the job and went on to win more games than any other major college coach.

The week after the Immaculate Reception, the Steelers lost the 1972 conference championship game against the Miami Dolphins. But that would be one of their few setbacks over the next decade.

Pittsburgh's defense, known as "The Steel Curtain," dominated the NFL. Led by Greene, Lambert, Ham, and Blount, the Steelers won their first Super Bowl in January 1975, beating the Minnesota Vikings 16-6. The Steelers won it all again the next year. Swann made a series of acrobatic catches to earn the game's Most Valuable Player (MVP) Award in a 21-17 victory over the Dallas Cowboys.

Steelers coach Chuck Noll holds the Lombardi Trophy after his team won its first Super Bowl.

Jack Lambert, *58*, was one of the fiercest members of the Steel Curtain defense.

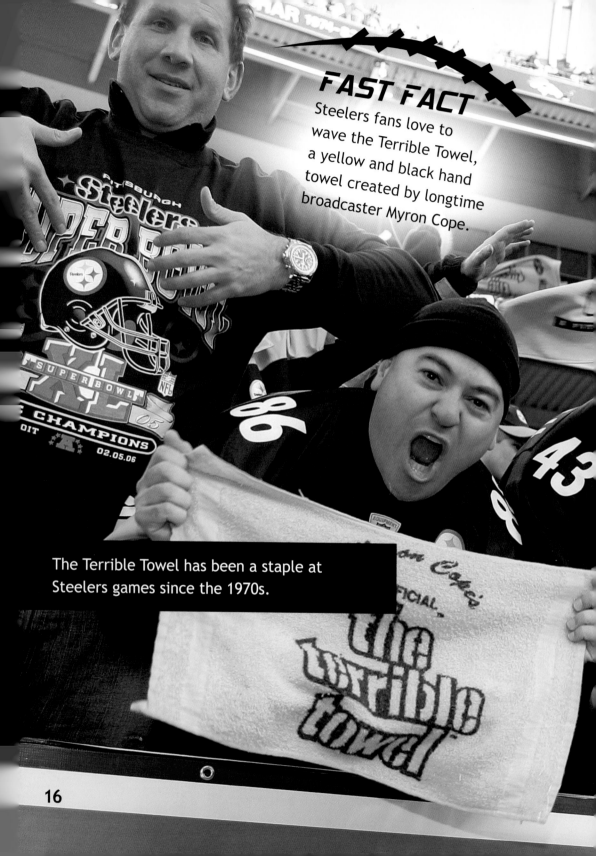

FAST FACT

Steelers fans love to wave the Terrible Towel, a yellow and black hand towel created by longtime broadcaster Myron Cope.

The Terrible Towel has been a staple at Steelers games since the 1970s.

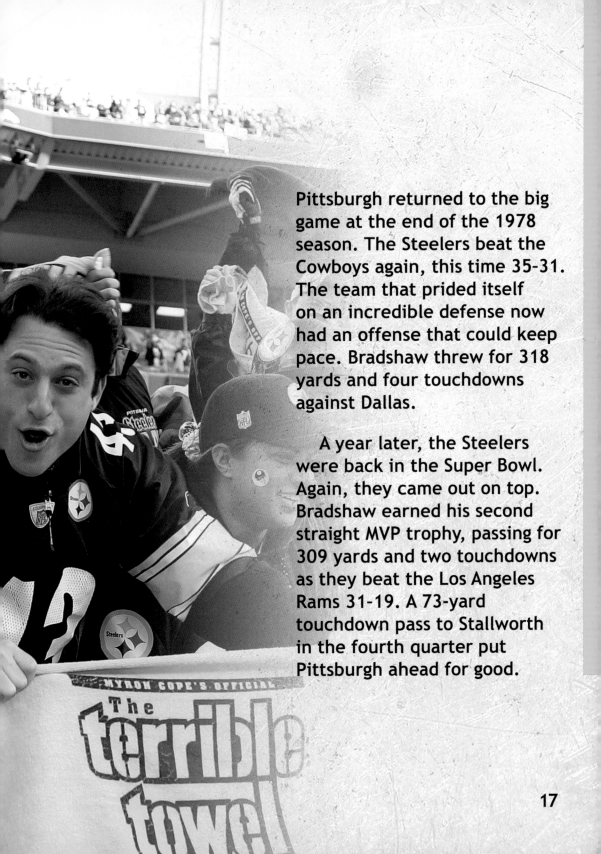

Pittsburgh returned to the big game at the end of the 1978 season. The Steelers beat the Cowboys again, this time 35-31. The team that prided itself on an incredible defense now had an offense that could keep pace. Bradshaw threw for 318 yards and four touchdowns against Dallas.

A year later, the Steelers were back in the Super Bowl. Again, they came out on top. Bradshaw earned his second straight MVP trophy, passing for 309 yards and two touchdowns as they beat the Los Angeles Rams 31-19. A 73-yard touchdown pass to Stallworth in the fourth quarter put Pittsburgh ahead for good.

The Steelers, losers for so many decades, won the Super Bowl four times in six years. No NFL team has been able to repeat that kind of success. The Steelers dominated the 1970s like few teams have dominated an era in any sport.

The Steelers called their attempt to get a fifth Super Bowl ring "One for the Thumb." It did not happen. Players got older and retired. The Steelers failed to make it back to the Super Bowl in the 1980s. Noll retired after the 1991 season. Two years later, he joined many of his former players in the Pro Football Hall of Fame.

Terry Bradshaw, *12*, launches a deep pass against the Los Angeles Rams in the Super Bowl.

FAST FACT
Terry Bradshaw and former Green Bay Packers quarterback Bart Starr are the only players to be named Super Bowl MVP two years in a row.

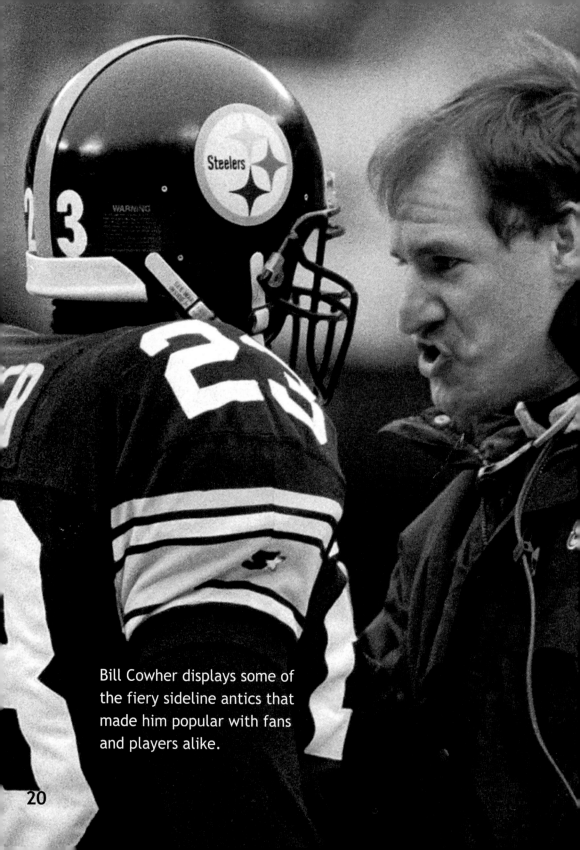

Bill Cowher displays some of the fiery sideline antics that made him popular with fans and players alike.

COWHER POWER

Bill Cowher was born only a few miles from Three Rivers Stadium in Pittsburgh. In 1992, the Steelers hired him as coach. At age 34, he was replacing a legend in Chuck Noll. Steelers fans expected him to get the team back to the Super Bowl.

Cowher made an immediate impact. He was very different from the stone-faced Noll on the sidelines. Cowher was always fired up. His players fed off their coach's energy, and it led to a return to greatness.

FAST FACT

Bill Cowher was the second NFL coach to lead his team to the playoffs in each of his first six seasons.

A Steelers fan appears to be in shock after his team lost to the Dallas Cowboys in the Super Bowl on January 28, 1996.

Thanks to a defense that at times played like the Steel Curtain of the 1970s, the Steelers got back to the Super Bowl at the end of the 1995 season. For the third time in 21 years, the Steelers and Cowboys squared off in the big game. This time, Dallas found a way to come out on top. Pittsburgh rallied from a 13-point deficit to pull to within 20-17 in the fourth quarter. But a late interception ended the comeback.

Over the next 10 seasons, the Steelers made it to the playoffs five times and the conference championship game three times. But it took a historic postseason run after the 2005 season to get them back to the Super Bowl.

Behind veteran running back Jerome "The Bus" Bettis and rookie quarterback Ben Roethlisberger, the Steelers became the first team in NFL history to win three playoff games on the road in the same year. That put them in the Super Bowl against the Seattle Seahawks.

Running back Willie Parker set a Super Bowl record with a 75-yard touchdown run. Wide receiver Hines Ward earned MVP honors by catching five passes for 123 yards. His 43-yard touchdown catch in the fourth quarter sealed a 21-10 victory. Bettis headed off into retirement after the game. Cowher joined him a year later, stepping away after a successful 15-year run in Pittsburgh.

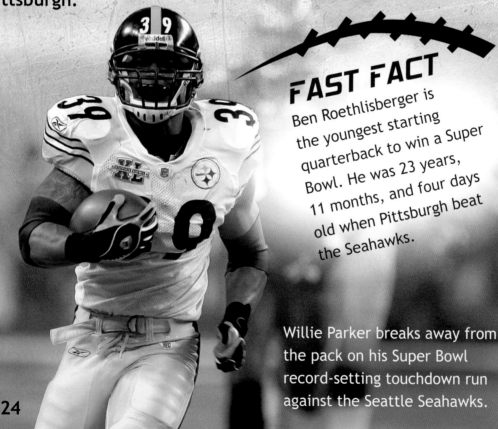

FAST FACT

Ben Roethlisberger is the youngest starting quarterback to win a Super Bowl. He was 23 years, 11 months, and four days old when Pittsburgh beat the Seahawks.

Willie Parker breaks away from the pack on his Super Bowl record-setting touchdown run against the Seattle Seahawks.

Super Bowl MVP Hines Ward, *left*, and Jerome Bettis embrace after the Steelers beat the Seahawks in February 2006.

25

TOMLIN TIME

Just as they did when they replaced Chuck Noll, the Steelers took a chance on a young coach to take over for Bill Cowher. Mike Tomlin was just 34 when Pittsburgh hired him in 2007. He was the defensive coordinator for the Minnesota Vikings at the time. He won the Steelers over with his smarts and his energy.

It did not take the players long to warm up to Tomlin. They kept on winning. Pittsburgh reached the Super Bowl for a seventh time at the end of the 2008 season. Hard-hitting safety Troy Polamalu and fearsome linebacker James Harrison led the NFL's best defense. Ben Roethlisberger directed an offense that made a habit of making big plays.

The Steelers quickly fell in line behind coach Mike Tomlin, *right*.

James Harrison, *right*, fights off Arizona's Larry Fitzgerald to score on a 100-yard interception return in the Super Bowl.

FAST FACT
James Harrison's 100-yard interception return was the longest defensive score in Super Bowl history.

The Steelers needed a big play with three minutes left in that Super Bowl. The Arizona Cardinals led 23-20. Roethlisberger marched his team down the field. On second down from the Arizona 6-yard line, he threw a perfect pass to the back corner of the end zone. Wide receiver Santonio Holmes caught it and tapped his toes in bounds for a touchdown. Pittsburgh had a 27-23 victory and a record sixth Super Bowl title.

Two years later, the Steelers were back in the Super Bowl but came up short against the Green Bay Packers. Still, thanks to stars such as wide receiver Antonio Brown and running back Le'Veon Bell, they remain one of the NFL's most consistent teams.

Santonio Holmes rejoices after his Super Bowl-winning touchdown catch.

Antonio Brown, *left*, and Ben Roethlisberger have put up big numbers together in Pittsburgh.

FAST FACT

Antonio Brown set an NFL record with 375 receptions between 2013 and 2015. No player has caught more passes over a three-year period in league history.

TIMELINE

1933
Art Rooney Sr. pays the NFL $2,500 to put a team in Pittsburgh.

1969
The Steelers hire 37-year-old Chuck Noll as coach. The team goes 1-13 during his first season but quickly improves.

1972
On December 23, Franco Harris makes the Immaculate Reception to lift the Steelers to a 13-7 win over the Oakland Raiders for the first playoff victory in team history.

1975
Pittsburgh defeats the Minnesota Vikings 16-6 on January 12 for its first Super Bowl title. Franco Harris is named MVP after running for 158 yards and a touchdown.

1976
The Steelers repeat as Super Bowl champions with a 21-17 victory over the Dallas Cowboys on January 18.

1979
Pittsburgh becomes the first team to win three Super Bowls, beating the Cowboys 35-31 on January 21.

1991
Noll retires with a career record of 209-156-1 and a record four Super Bowls.

2006
Pittsburgh defeats the Seattle Seahawks 21-10 on February 5 to win the team's fifth Super Bowl.

2009
The Steelers become the first team to win six Super Bowls, rallying past the Arizona Cardinals 27-23 on February 1.

GLOSSARY

ACROBATIC
Spectacular or showy, involving great agility.

CONTENDER
A team with a realistic chance at winning a championship.

COORDINATOR
An assistant coach who is in charge of a team's offense or defense.

CUT
When a player is removed from a team's roster.

DRAFT
The process by which teams select players who are new to the league.

INTERCEPTION
When a defensive player catches a pass intended for an offensive player.

LINEBACKER
A defensive player who usually lines up behind the defensive linemen.

ROOKIE
A first-year player.

INDEX

ABOUT THE AUTHOR

Will Graves grew up in Maryland fearing the Pittsburgh Steelers while cheering for Washington. He has spent more than 20 years as a sports writer and author. He lives in Pittsburgh and covers sports for The Associated Press.